WHAT I MISS

by
Harold E. Grice

Park Place Publications
Pacific Grove, California

Park Place Publications
Pacific Grove, California 93950
www.parkplacepublications.com

First Paperback Edition: October 2014

ISBN 978-1-935530-90-9

Printed in the USA

DEDICATION

To all kindred souls

Table of Contents

WHAT I MISS

What I miss of times gone by ...
   the sound of 78 records with a song
   short but understood before gone
     a blend of sounds in harmony
     the whole given melody
     ... to sing while milking cow

And things seen and heard ...
   "Indian Love Song" and fire fall
   John Deere smoke rings pulling plow
     bike chain rattle on pant leg guard
     evening melody of swamp frog
     ... all gone but the frog

And being able to tell on the road ...
   make of car by shape and front
   instead of being a similar lump
     hot rod motor and rumble of pipes
     giving mom jitters and dad jealous gripes
     ... creating desire for a "ROD"

And melancholy things gone from life ...
   long family dinners which could last
   through stories of humor and being fast
      aunts, uncles, relatives galore
      telling tales that are now lore
      ... each repeat better every time

And what is missing from the past ...
   relatives, friends, guys hanging around
   moved, gone off or underground
      places gone, changed, things made new
      can't go back to the haunts we knew
      ... change is for the better, it is said

But what I miss most of all, is ...
   tap, tap, high heels on the walk, tap, tap
   flash of comely ankle under strap
      a swish of skirt, a whiff of perfume
      the essence of a girl in the room
      ... in love, in love so many times

MUSIC IS FEELING, dreams of this and that, here and there, driving hard, falling in love, herding cows, flying high, melancholy, girls in the night, blue eyes and deserts and love. Music is the expression of an emotion, a memory or a dream in harmony and words. Having grown up listening to my sister and cousin practicing the violin and piano, I developed an appreciation for music. Listening to the car radio (at the ranch, before electricity, there were times we had to get the car out of the garage and push it to start and recharge the battery because we had listened too long). Then, going to town, we kids would sign the songs we heard. Sure, we weren't all that good, but at least we knew the melody and the tune.

There was always a song for whatever task you were doing: for digging fence post holes, "I've Been Working on the Railroad"; around the campfire, "Smoke Gets in Your Eyes"; driving the team, "She'll Be Coming around the Mountain"; herding cows, "Git Along Little Dogie"; and milking cows, anything melancholy until she switches you in the eye with her tail, then anything with curses in it.

The songs of today just don't do that for me, so it is best I listen to the records with the music I know and enjoy.

"Come a Ki Yi Yippee Yippee Yay" under "Blue Skies" to "Red Sails in the Sunset" and "My Desert Is Waiting" where you can be a "Hound Dog."

HEARING THE JOHN DEERE let us know the neighbor farm was being tilled. Hearing the crack of a rifle told us someone was hunting in the valley; the pop of a shotgun spoke of bird shooting. Cows bawling meant someone was pushing a herd from here to there. Dogs yapping meant they were chasing something (probably one of the cats). Sounds were messages of happenings.

Spring was special with the scent of new blossoms, wild flowers, fruit tree blooms and berry vines. Turned earth has a scent, as do the new shoots of the willows, oak trees and new grass coming from the ground. These all meant it was spring, and time to get to work. No more sitting by the pot-bellied stove reading one of Mother's books, or whittling images of animals or clowns or other people in the wood that would end up in the fire anyway.

That world is gone: brakes don't screech; wheels don't squeak (sqqueeeaak-needs some grease); and the John Deere doesn't chugga – chugga – chugga chugg poooff anymore.

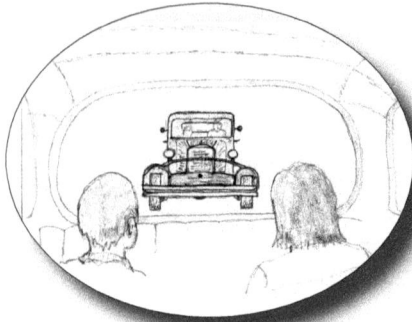

THERE WAS A FINITE type of cars and after a while each was familiar. Then came the straight 6, the straight 8 and then the V8, and even a V12 in a Lincoln Zephyr. These we all knew. We could stand along the road and watch the cars go by, each one familiar. There were two-door and four-door models, and some with rumble seats. Some chugged and some popped and ground gears when shifting. There were lines of cars following one another and then there would be a wild one passing everyone.

The Burma Shave signs, always fun, always a pun:

THE LIGHTS WERE LIT

AND SO WAS HE

ENDED UP IN A TREE

WHERE HE FOUND

ETERNITY

— BURMA SHAVE

Now, with models and varieties from all over the world, it is difficult to know the make, model or what's under the hood.

Ah, for the good old days.

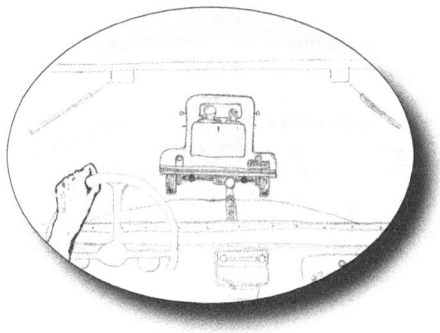

FAMILY GATHERINGS OCCURRED on a
regular basis with aunts, uncles and cousins galore present.
Before we went to the ranch, it was Dad and uncles doing
barbecue (I'm not sure they called it barbecue). It was as often
as not done on chicken wire, with the galvanizing burned off
first, as with a regular grate. After Dad died and Mom remarried
and we went to the ranch, Brown, my stepfather, built a regular
barbecue. It was, like most every improvement at the ranch, aided
greatly by uncles' help. Everyone would stand around and BS, tell
stories of great shots and big horns and quail or dove on the wing
while the meat was cooking. As often as not it was side hill salmon,
that is, venison obtained out of season. Then after us kids left the
ranch, it was at my aunt Mary Jane's or one of the uncle's.

But always there was lots of food and stories.
One of my favorite storytellers was Grandma Emert.
She told of crossing the plains in a covered wagon and bouncing
so much her bones hurt. It was actually a relief when it was slow
enough going that as a little girl she could keep up walking. One
of their most prized and admired possessions was a chair that the
ladies would take turns sitting in.

In the summer we often went to the beach, Avila, and had hotdogs
with things folks brought, salad and stuff. Spent a lot of time in the
water—boy was it cold. Stay in until you shivered so bad you couldn't
stand it then go lie in the sun until you warmed up, then go jump in
again.

REMEMBER WHEN THINGS were simple and you could know everything? When questions of what was believed were dismissed without thinking And the hangouts populated with others of like mind or known conflict? Then how to be tough without actually fighting the bums was the trick. Things aren't like that anymore.

Remember the jukebox, the drinks, the girls and guys we knew well? Now where are they? A few we see, the others in ground, some in hell. Or the bar where we used to go? It's gone like them, just a dark window. Or the line of trees where we'd spoon? Now just storefronts in a row. Things aren't like that anymore.

It's sad to think of the things now gone that the present seems to lack, which made our world the place to be, but in all truth, I wouldn't go back.

We remember only the best of times. And the best of times is tomorrow.

Before Mother died, Saturday nights were a movie for us kids then down to the Grange Hall dance where they did the waltz, rounds, fox trot, two step and rounds with Allemande left and swing your partner round and round thrown in for spice. The violinist had to tune the fiddle all the time, the trumpet player kept it quiet, usually, and the drummer seemed to be asleep most of the time and seldom heard from. But the lady played the piano with gusto and tape on her fingers and carried the score. And she could make that old piano rattle when she wanted to.

GIRLS—GIRLS TO BRIGHTEN TIME, be friend or not
Girls—silken skin, active body in loose frock
Imagination imaging that which is or is not
Building expectation, seduced by thought.

Girls in skirt, silken legs flashing,
Tap of heels on the walk, passing
Good solid walk from the sound,
Pleasuring shape, up and down,
In her wake comes the fume,
The heady fragrance of perfume.

Girls are nice with shoulder bare,
Soft of skin, nice soft looking hair
I'd really like to meet this girl,
Have a dance, take a whirl.
Can I talk, keep it fun?
Seems like the cat gets my tongue
But just don't let her go on by,
I'll never know unless I try

She's a sweetheart, now goodbye.

H.E.Cruce
14 -06/09

ENTERTAINMENT by

CALIFORNIA COUNTRY BOY

Harold E. Grice

www.ingramcontent.com/pod-product-compliance
Lightning Source LLC
Chambersburg PA
CBHW060607030426
42337CB00019B/3648